My
First Holy
Communion
Album

YOUCAT for Kids

From the bottom of our hearts
we wish you all happiness and blessings
on your First Holy Communion.

My First Holy Communion Album

YOUCAT for Kids

CATHOLIC TRUTH SOCIETY

Bob and Lilly and their First Holy Communion

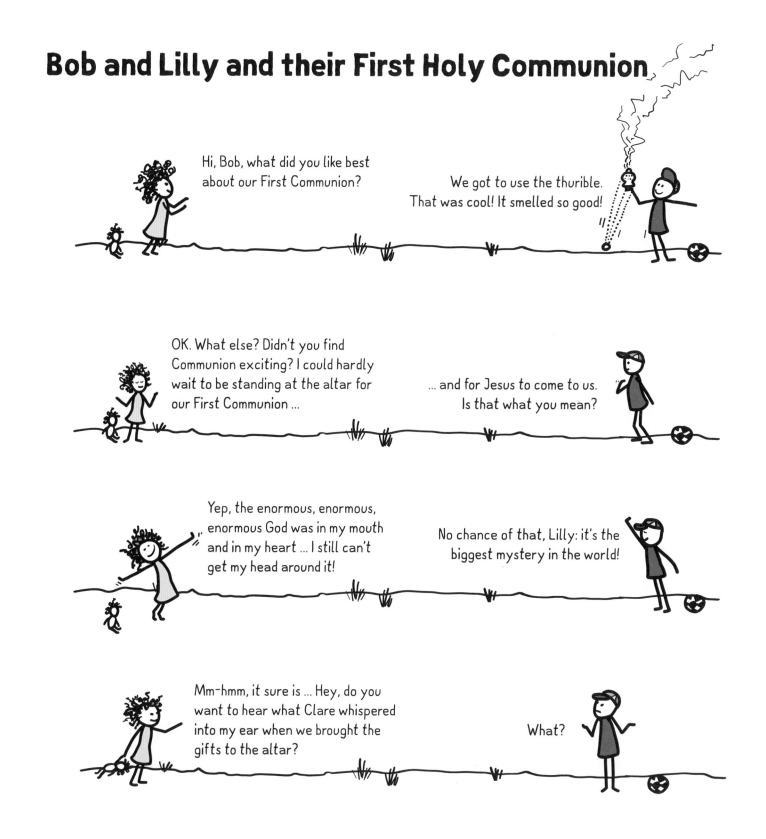

The Profile of
JESUS

Name: Jesus of Nazareth

Mother: Mary

Foster father: Joseph the Carpenter

Birthday: Christmas day. You celebrate my birthday on the 25th December, which is OK with me. Most scholars say I was born seven years earlier (7 BC). That's fine too! But what's really cool is that, at my birth, a new calendar began. Did you know that?

Place of birth: Bethlehem in Judaea

Profession: Carpenter

Languages: Mother tongue: Aramaic; First learnt language: Hebrew

Outdoor activities: Walking, sailing, mountain climbing

What I like: Being with children; celebrating festivals, but I also enjoy being alone sometimes; my friends; having my feet anointed; healing diseases and forgiving sins; talking to my father in heaven; talking with people about God

What annoys me: When my people are divided into various groups, poor and rich, pious and not so pious, and don't live as God wants them to any longer

My greatest moment: Oh, there are so many ... How about the time I turned water into wine at a wedding, after my mother pointed out that there was none left ... The absolute highlight was my resurrection. I'm alive!

My motto: "Change your life now, for God is already very close!"

What I like about you: I'd really like us to get to know each other better here and now!

My PROFILE

You can stick your photo in here (2.3 × 3.0 cm)

Name: _____

Mother: _____

Father: _____

Birthday: _____

Place of birth: _____

When I grow up, I want to be: _____

Languages I want to learn: _____

Outdoor activities: _____

What I like: _____

_____

_____

What annoys me: _____

_____

_____

My greatest moment: _____

_____

My motto: _____

What I like about Jesus: _____

_____

_____

Photos of my best friends

Bob
is always on
the lookout for
new pranks.

Lilly

knows the funniest jokes in the whole world.

The story of how Jesus made a lot of friends

You're might think Jesus was alone, but you'd be wrong: he had no lack of friends, and I can tell you how it all began.

At the very beginning

Jesus had a relative, John, the Baptist. He was a prophet, that's someone who fiercely tells people the truth. John was tough: he lived outdoors in the desert with wild animals, he wore a shaggy garment made of camel hair and lived on locusts and wild honey. People found their way to him, even though he was not one to flatter them, "Hey, you are the worst of sinners! You need to change your lives completely!" There were many people who said, "Whew, he is right!" And they were baptised as a sign to show that they wanted to start a new life.

Was it him or not?

John was so famous that some thought, "He must be the Messiah!" Now, what does the word "Messiah" mean? It is Hebrew and means something like "anointed one" (= king) or saviour. The people of Israel had been yearning for the Messiah, and they thought, "It's John! He is the man who is going to throw those stupid Romans out of the country and make Israel great again." But John said, "You're barking up the wrong tree. I'm nothing compared to the one who is coming. I'm not even worthy to untie the straps of his sandals!" And he pointed at Jesus.

Curiosity mounted

Let's check this out! Two of John's followers went after Jesus until he turned around: "Are you searching for something?" What should they say? It was awkward. "Let's try addressing him as 'rabbi' (= teacher)", they thought. And they said,

"Rabbi, where do you live?" Jesus probably had a smile on his face when he said, "Well, come and see!" That's what they did; and they didn't just stay for the whole day – they stayed for ever.

One of them was called Andrew. He couldn't wait to run to the fishing harbour to tell his brother Simon the news, "Hey, hey … we've found him!!!" – "Who?" – "The Messiah!" Simon, of course, didn't need to be told twice. He came to Jesus and stayed. That was amazing since he had a fishing company. Imagine what his crew, who were perhaps sorting fish, must have said when their "boss" told them, "You have

to do this on your own now. I have to go away with Jesus!" Well, it didn't take long for him to become the "boss" in Jesus's crew as well.

Things then moved quickly

The next day, Jesus wanted to set off from the Jordan – which, by the way, is the lowest point on the earth's surface – up to the hill country of Galilee. That's where he bumped into Philip. They had a chat, and Jesus said, "Come, follow me!" And he did. But Philip did not come alone – he brought Nathanael with him. Have you kept count? That already makes five …

Just imagine what a huge troupe must have arrived in Galilee together with Jesus, and without the slightest self-promotion. He could also have said, "I'm the greatest – and you are going to have a lot of success. Money and all that!" That's precisely what he did not do. He even said, "I'm warning you that if you come with me, foxes have dens and birds have nests, where it's cosy, but I can't offer you any of that. Therefore, consider carefully if you want to join me!" Some of his first friends – the Bible also calls them "disciples" – certainly went back home: "Sorry, Jesus, but that's too much of a risk …" Imagine if they had made a film of it back then.

How do we arm ourselves?

Scene 1: They stop at a well: ah! water and shade! They fill their bowls and sit down on the ground. All eyes are on Jesus, who is sitting at the edge of the well and quenches his thirst too. "Hey," one of them exclaims, "now tell us where we are heading and what we are supposed to do. Where do we get weapons from?" Jesus is shaking his head: "Oh, guys, you still don't get it. My father in heaven has sent me to you to bring good news to the poor. God wants the best for them. Whoever is blind now, will see. Whoever is bound now, will be set free." The disciples probably had no idea of what he was talking about. "And what's our job in all of this?"

At the risk of their lives …

Scene 2: A few weeks later: the friends have begun to understand Jesus better. Jesus picks out some of them: "You! … You too! The two of you over there … and you with the red hair!" In the end, it's seventy people he comes back with – into, let's say, a cave where they all can hear him well: "Listen. I'm sending you, two by two, into the villages to tell the people, 'The kingdom of God is very near!' But do be careful: I'm sending you like harmless sheep into the land of wolves." – "But Jesus! don't we need weapons?" – "No! Don't take anything with you, not even a money bag."

So they did just that. A few days later they came back. "And, how did it go?" Jesus asked. "Amazing!" one of them said, "We were almost working wonders. And nothing happened to us!" "You're my friends!"

From now on you're my friends

Scene 3: Jesus said something incredible to his disciples: "I shall not call you servants any more, because a servant does not know his master's business; I call you friends …" Wow! That was like being promoted to the Premier League, and so much more. For what is a friend?

A friend is someone I don't keep secrets from. A friend is someone I can trust one hundred percent, because I've tested him one hundred times. And even if something happens, a friend comes and says, "I've got a confession to make, even if you're going to despise me after that ..."

Now you might say that these are just some old stories. No, they're not! Jesus is still searching today for real friends ready to go through thick and thin with him. Going to communion means you say to Jesus,

> **Yes, I'm your friend. I want to connect with you deeply!**

My friendship makes you strong against evil!

Gossip! Scratch! Bite!

I want to love people as much as I love myself!

I want to make sure no one feels lonely.

I want to have a pure heart!

I want to make peace when I see two people quarrelling.

Don't listen to Jesus! He is the biggest spoilsport in the world.

Take what you can get. Then you are the greatest!

I want to forgive someone sincerely, as if nothing had happened!

Think of YOURSELF only!

I'm proud if someone points a finger at me: "She/He is a Christian. They even go to church."

I resolve to not talk badly about others.

Be smart and phoney, devious and evil.

I want to talk with Jesus every day (= pray), thank him and ask him to help me lead a good life.

I have something against Jesus, because I'm THE DEVIL!

It's good to have a friend

Some people have a thousand friends;
Good and bad ones;
Others have none at all.
Maybe because they are not tall enough, not strong enough,
not smart enough for everyone to want to be their friend.

God saw that.

And because it just cannot be
that there is even one single person on earth
who doesn't have a friend, he sent his own son
and said to him:
"You be the best friend
in the whole world!"
And when you see someone

being sad: be his friend!
And when you see someone
being lonely: be his friend!
And when you see someone
no one likes: show him
that you like him!
Jesus did that;

He still does;

And he is asking you and me,

"Do you need a friend?

Yes?

Then come! I'm there for you!"

Friends

... laugh together.

... encourage each other.

... have secrets together.

... stick together through thick and thin.

... share with each other.

... celebrate together.

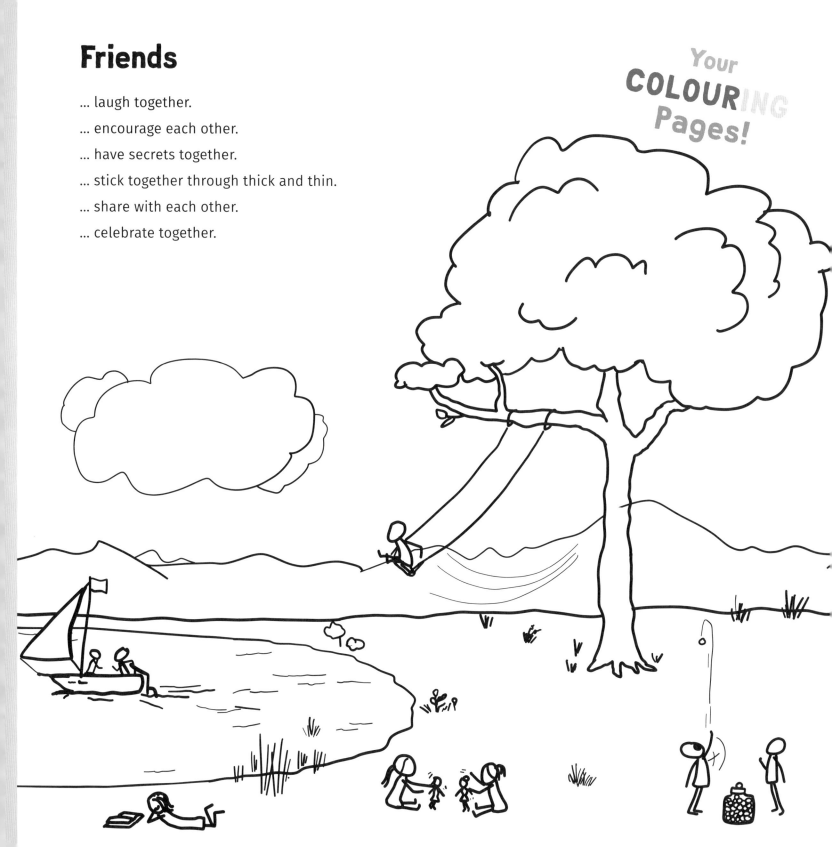

Your friendship with Jesus

Tell him what makes you happy;

Trust him with things you wouldn't tell anyone else;

Share with him what bothers you and what you are afraid of;

Ask him to give you strength where you are weak;

Go to him when he invites you to come, every Sunday, to his big feast, the Holy Mass.

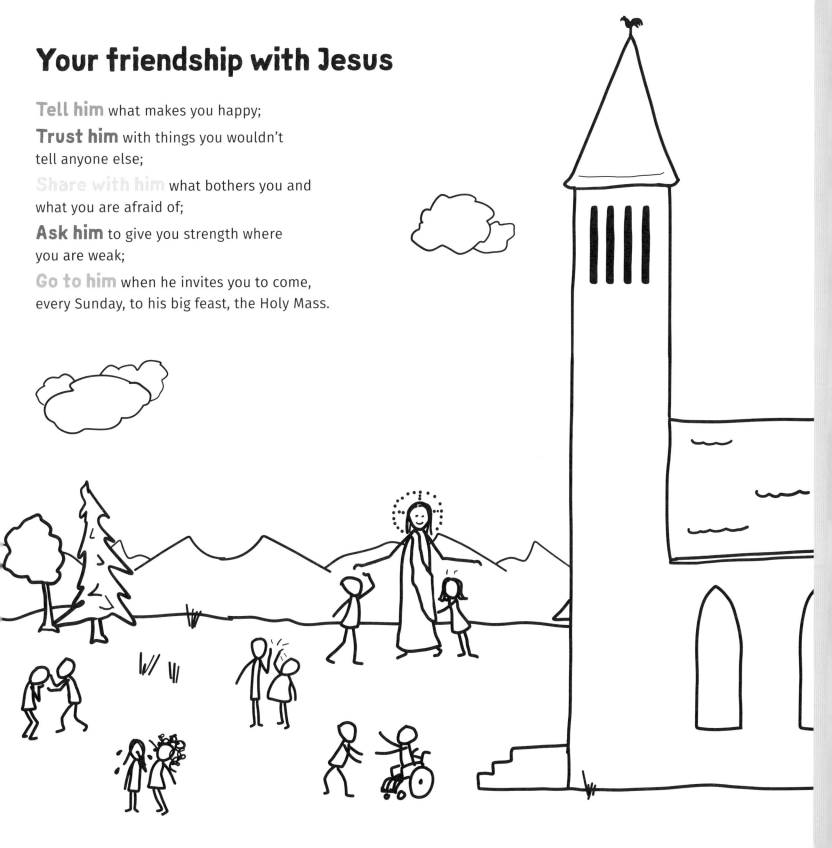

Photos of you entering the church

Let's read again why it is so important to go to Holy Mass and receive Holy Communion:

75 *What happens at Holy Mass?*

The Holy Mass is a miracle:
we can be present at
Jesus's death and resurrection.
With Jesus Christ, our risen Lord,
we are celebrating the big feast
of → thanksgiving.

At the → Passover Festival
Jesus died. He died for us all.
The evening before, Jesus held
a last supper with his disciples and
celebrated the great thanksgiving.
He offered them → bread and wine
and in doing so, he spoke the
unfathomable words:

This is my Body

→ The Greek word for thanksgiving is "Eucharist". Eucharist is another name for Holy Mass.

→ The Passover Festival (in Hebrew, *Pesach* – pronounced Pei-sach) is the Jewish feast that recalls the exodus of the people of Israel from Egypt.

→ The bread used in the Holy Mass is also called the host after the consecration. Host comes from the Latin *hostia* = sacrifice, oblation.

→ "To communicate" comes from the Latin *communio* (= union, community). That is why we call receiving the Body and Blood of Christ Communion. We become one with Jesus Christ and are united with our sisters and brothers.

In the Mass, the priest repeats those exact words over the bread and wine. Through the Holy Spirit, the bread and wine become Jesus's Body and Jesus's Blood.

In each Holy Mass
Jesus's death and resurrection
are made present for us:
we meet the crucified and resurrected Lord
and unite ourselves with him,
by going to Communion (= → to communicate).

It's not like on TV,
when we watch a film
for the thousandth time.
Through Holy Mass
we experience the death
and resurrection of Jesus live.

... This is my Blood.

Photos of us around the altar

Just like my candle, I too want to ...

BRING LIGHT,

where people have
dark thoughts.

GIVE WARMTH,

where people are cold and
hard to each other.

SPREAD JOY,

where people are sad and have
forgotten how to smile.

Most of all, I want
to be as tall as
my candle one day.

My friend and Lord Jesus Christ,

give me the strength to live a life that radiates,

because I treat people and God's creatures well.

Give me that kind of life that spreads light,

because I am thankful for my parents,

my home, my body and my skills.

I believe in you and know:

you yourself are **the** true light

that dispels the darkness from the world

and brings bright joy. Amen!

You can stick in a nice
photo of you and your
candle here!
10 x 15 cm

Photos of the festive day

Photos of the festive day

Photos of the festive day

Photos of the festive day

Photos of the festive day

The evening has come and I now have time to reflect ...

What was I thinking when I got up on the morning of my First Communion?

_____

_____

_____

What did I feel when we entered the church?

_____

_____

What did the priest say in his sermon?

_____

_____

_____

What was I thinking when I received the Body and Blood of the Lord for the first time?

_____

_____

_____

When did I laugh really hard?

_____

_____

_____

What was the gift I was most excited about?

_____

_____

What did I like best of all the festive food?

_____

_____

Which guest had to travel very far to see me?

_____

_____

_____

What was the most beautiful moment of the whole day?

_____

_____

_____

What is it that I don't want to forget about my special day for the rest of my life?

_____

_____

_____

The little guest book

We were your guests at your First Communion ...

my deerest Norah
Congratulations on your Communion dey
mey you + Jesus enjoy every
adventure together love Caroline
x + x

Norah,
what a wonderful day for you.
Congratulations + you're a great
girl!! love Jen.

Dear Norah,
Lovely occasion, enjoyed it
very much! from Bob!!

I wish you a super
awesome
mega-friendship
with Jesus!

All the best,
Bob

NORAH CONG GRATS
ON YOUR HOLY COMMUNION.
YOU LOOK FAB. TODAY
LOVE AND BEST WISH
GRANDAD & GRANNY
x x x x x

NORAH you a beautiful I so happy
For you Thank for haven us I love
you so much God Bless Love you
Margaret John

♡ Norah, I have never been so proud as I was of you today. #HedgehogPhoto. Love Mummy ♡ xx

and **these** are our heartfelt wishes:

Dear Norah,
wishing you a fabulous day on your first holy communion.
we are enjoying the lovely food & your cousins are having lots of fun on the bouncy castle in the dark!
Susan, Shane, Graeme, Robyn
Hayley & Olivia xx

Norah,
Hope you a brilliant day, loved the dress and the sings
lots of love
Sinead Hannah.
P.S. Thanks for inviting us, Hannah is having a fab time.

happy communion day Norah love from
Robyn x x

Dear Norah
Hope you enjoy your very special communion day, and you will always Remember Holy God is always with you
with love Noirie & Sean xx

THANKS GUYS! from Norah

My wish for you is that you let go of all fear, because God loves you so much and is always with you!
love, Lilly

Thank you for being with me!

Jesus Christ,

my dear Lord and God,

you have invited me.

I was allowed to get closer to you than ever before.

I have taken you inside me

and I carry you in my heart.

You are mine, and I am yours.

How beautiful is that?

I praise you and I thank you

for being so good to me.

Oh yes – and I thank you

for giving me parents

and so many other wonderful people,

who love me with all their heart

and accompany me in my life.

Thank you for ... [Here you can think of names and tell them to Jesus!]

Bless them and make them happy.

Jesus Christ!

I carry your name

and I am proud

to be a Christian.

Help me, through your Holy Spirit,

so I don't make anybody sad.

Help me to bring joy into the world

and be good to everyone

who needs me.

AMEN.

A place for your thank you card

Hmm ... becoming an altar server? A great thing!

You've received your First Holy Communion.
Bingo!

If you want, you can now become an altar girl or
an altar boy!
Seriously? Of course!
And what do they do?

- Altar servers help the priest during Mass.
- They make sure everything's alright with the chalice, the paten, the prayer books, the candles, the bells and the incense.
- On important feasts, such as Easter, Pentecost and Christmas, the altar servers and the priest often enter the church with twenty people. Totally festive!

Simply register!

Your parish priest will be happy for you to join in!

_____   _____

Imprint

Published by The Incorporated Catholic Truth Society,
42-46 Harleyford Road, London SE11 5AY
English Edition © 2019 The Incorporated Catholic Truth Society.

Bibliographic information of the German National Library.
The German National Library registers this publication in the German National
Bibliography; detailed bibliographic information can be found on the internet via
http://dnb.dnb.de

Idea and implementation by Bernhard Meuser, Claudia Weiß and
Alexander von Lengerke

German Edition © 2019 not-for-profit YOUCAT Foundation GmbH.
Sole shareholder of the YOUCAT Foundation is the papal charity ACN with
headquarters in Königstein in Taunus, Germany. All rights reserved. The name
YOUCAT is used with permission of the YOUCAT Foundation. YOUCAT® is an
internationally protected trademark. Registered under GM: 011929131

Cover design, layout, illustrations and typesetting by Alexander von Lengerke,
Cologne, Germany
Printed and bound by Gomer Press Ltd
Produced by Druckmedien Speyer GmbH in co-operation with
Parzeller print & media GmbH & Co. KG
Production co-ordination by Druckmedien Speyer GmbH, Speyer

ISBN: 978-1-78469-619-1
www.youcat.org From the proceeds of its publications and from donations,
the not-for-profit YOUCAT Foundation GmbH supports worldwide projects of new
evangelisation, encouraging young people to discover the Christian faith as a
foundation for their lives. You can help further the work of the YOUCAT Foundation
with your donations, which can be made through: Deutsche Bank AG, BCN 720 700
24, Account No: 031 888 100, IBAN: DE13 7207 0024 0031 8881 00, BIC: DEUTDEDB720

Picture Credits

Felipe Belloni; Martine Boutros; Charles Costantine; Thomas Crouzier; Ildikò von
Ketteler; Mattia Mohr; Father Jude Thaddeus Langeh; Alexander von Lengerke;
Pixabay, licensed CC0 1.0; Albus Pioquinto; Peter Rydzon, Jodi Stauffer
p. 17 Waiting for the Word, *www.flickr.com*